WIND

SCIENCE SECRETS

Jason Cooper

The Rourke Corporation, Inc.
Vero Beach, Florida 32964

Edited by Sandra A. Robinson

PHOTO CREDITS

© Lynn M. Stone: Title page, pages 4, 12, 13, 15; © Jerry Hennen:
page 10; courtesy NOAA, pages 17, 18, 21; courtesy NASA, page 7;
courtesy Star Clippers, Coral Gables, Florida, page 8; © James P.
Rowan, cover

LIBRARY OF CONGRESS
Library of Congress Cataloging-in-Publication Data
Cooper, Jason, 1942-
    Wind / by Jason Cooper.
    p. cm. — (Science secrets)
    Includes index.
    Summary: Provides a simple discussion of the causes of air
movement, uses of wind power, and such phenomena as hurricanes
and tornadoes.
    ISBN 0-86593-171-2
    1. Winds—Juvenile literature. [1. Winds.]
I. Title. II. Series: Cooper, Jason, 1942-   Science secrets.
QC931.4.C66   1992
551.5'18—dc20
                                        92-8811
                                           CIP
                                           AC

TABLE OF CONTENTS

WIND

In a story written long ago, the wind lives in a palace. It speaks and it sometimes grants wishes.

The real wind, however, is no more than a movement, or motion, of air. We cannot see the wind, but we can see what it does and feel its force. And sometimes it does seem to speak, with a soft whisper or a loud howl.

A howling sea wind

WHAT MAKES THE WIND?

Air covers the earth's surface. Air is the tasteless, odorless substance that we breathe.

Air can be dry or wet, hot or cold. Think of each kind of air as a bubble. The air bubbles move. For example, a hot air bubble rises. As it does, a cold air bubble moves to take its place.

This movement of air bubbles helps to make wind. The earth's spinning motion in space also makes air movement.

Planet earth viewed from space

TRADE WINDS

In some parts of the world, the wind almost always blows. It usually blows from the same direction, too.

Some of the steady winds that blow over oceans are known as **trade winds.** They used to help sailing ships move swiftly across the sea. These ships traded goods from one country to another.

Trade winds still push modern clipper ships

WIND ENERGY

The wind is a bit like a butterfly. It seems to come and go as it pleases. And the wind is like a wild horse—full of **energy.**

The energy of moving air, the wind, is a powerful force. By catching the wind, we can use its energy, or power, for our purposes.

Windmills use wind's energy

Wind stirs flags of many nations

Wind energy helps lift pelican

WINDMILLS

Windmills are built especially to catch the wind's energy. Windmills are made in many sizes and styles, but all of them have sails or paddles for the wind to push.

As the wind pushes the sails or paddles, the windmill's parts move. The windmill can then pump water or power a machine that makes electricity.

Dutch-style windmill

MEASURING THE WIND

A **weather vane** turns in the wind and shows from which direction—north, south, east or west—the wind is blowing.

An **anemometer** measures how fast the wind blows. The wind at ground level may blow at a different speed and from a different direction than the wind above it.

Both weather vanes and anemometers help people predict the weather.

Anemometer at National Hurricane Center, Florida

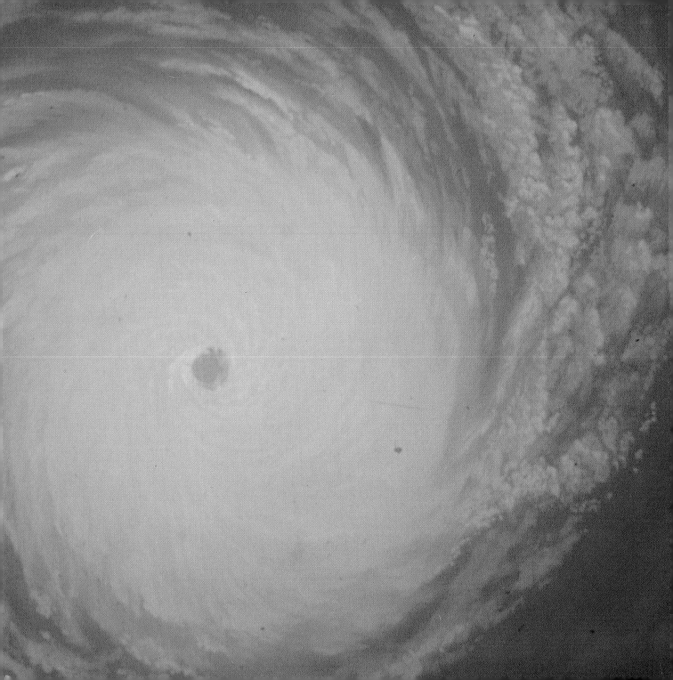

HURRICANES

When an anemometer shows the wind speed at 75 miles per hour or above, the wind is blowing at **hurricane** force.

A hurricane is a powerful, wet storm that builds over warm sea water. Most hurricanes in the United States form in the Atlantic Ocean.

Like a top, a hurricane whirls as it moves forward. But the center, or **eye,** is calm.

A hurricane may be 450 miles across and last nearly two weeks as it travels over hundreds of miles. It can cause terrible damage.

Artist's view of hurricane and eye

TORNADOES

Unlike a hurricane, a tornado usually lasts less than one hour, and its path is usually no wider than the length of a football field.

A tornado is a violent, whirling wind storm that develops in thunderclouds. It appears as a black, funnel-shaped cloud dipping toward earth.

When a tornado strikes ground, it usually destroys everything in its path. The wind speed of a tornado is probably several hundred miles per hour inside the funnel.

A dipping, twisting tornado

MORE WIND STORMS

Sometimes tornadoes form over water. They are known as **waterspouts.**

Tropical depressions are hard, wet storms with wind nearing hurricane force. They happen only in very warm areas, like southern Florida.

Sand storm winds stir up dust and sand in dry, desert regions. Because a sand storm carries this material as it passes, it can make daytime almost as dark as night.

Glossary

anemometer (an eh MOM eh ter) — an instrument that measures and shows wind speed

energy (EN er gee) — power; the ability to do work

eye (I) — the calm center of a hurricane

hurricane (HER uh kane) — a powerful wind storm with heavy rains and a wind speed of at least 75 miles per hour

trade winds (TRAYD wihnds) — a group of steady winds that blow from east to west along one path and from west to east along another

tropical depression (TRAHP uh kul duh PRESH un) — hard, wet storms of warm regions, with winds nearing 75 miles per hour

waterspout (WAW ter spout) — a tornado over a large body of water

weather vane (WEH ther VANE) — a device used to tell wind direction

INDEX